Real Estate Investing

The Blueprint to Starting a Passive Income Business and Making Money Through Rental Optimization and Property Management

Timothy Turner

Table of contents

Introduction

Through business papers, radio, and television, we constantly see news or analysis that has to do with real estate. You may be wondering why this is happening and how can real estate be such a blooming and sure business despite the global economic crisis. The truth is that real estate is a sure investment despite the occasional downs it suffers. For instance, house flipping which is the practice of buying real estate, improving it, and selling it again for a higher price, has been very popular throughout the past ten years as an investment; however, it has been around for more than that.

Would you believe me if I told you, the practice of real estate investment dates back to the Revolutionary War? Even before that, we could imagine that cave drawings were a form of real estate investing. Even though Homo erectus did not rent out caves to other tribes, historians do maintain that a currency exchange of shorts existed among the early humans for them to gain shelter. In various agrarian systems, fertile lands were marked by settlers and those who were able to defend the land were able to keep it.

As time passed the system of tribal leaders was developed and those who were appointed by the tribe could disperse lands, ask for payments, and settle disputes. When stronger tribal leaders emerged, strongholds were created as well as temples, irrigation channels and farming methods were improved. This actually meant that farmers were then able to support more children and thus the increase in fertility meant greater numbers of workers. On the other hand, families that were focused on hunting were able to support two children at best. The people who were hunters followed a tribal system too but suffered because of uncertainty in life and scarcity. That was translated to them being able to support only two or three at most extended families.

Farmers soon realized that they could not protect their tribe's territory effectively from raiders. For this reason, they sacrificed their tribe's community to gain the safety of numbers. They joined the protection of an army controlled by a king and all paid homage to him who claimed the ownership of the land. This was the first system of rent, in its most basic form. Those villages of farmers turned to cities with the original leading families kept their ownership due to their right of lineage since their ancestors were the ones who protected the tribe from raiders.

The system that was then developed, labor in exchange for protection, was separated into two different systems in the majority of countries and included tenancy and taxes. The royal family gave to those who were loyal to them, wealth, titles, and deeds to lands. Those deeds allowed those who had them to collect money from the subjects that lived there, essentially they collected rent. Aside from this rent, everyone that lived within the borders of a ruler's territory had to pay taxes.

Various other demands were made by rulers such as military service and the people could rarely do something because those who governed did so not only by birthright but also because of their strong military. Even though rulers could be overthrown by other kings and sometimes by the people, another would take the throne and the average people most times would not notice anything different.

However, things were not that bleak since they were able to indulge in trading with other kingdoms. As the level of wealth increased for the people too, a class of merchants was created that included specialized tradesmen and laborers who could make ends meet not through farming but through skill. As a result, shops, as well as houses, emerged that had nothing to do with farming that still paid the required taxes and rent to the landlords and kings, however, they were rented, bought, and sold among commoners and not only by those who belonged to royalty. Rich merchants were the first landlords who were not royalty but commoners, thus gaining status and wealth among others. Even though those merchants did not own the land, they owned the houses included in these lands.

As time passed and aristocracies were replaced by accepted meritocracies, systems through which the smartest and best ruled a nation for the good of the people, politics as we know them today began to form. The titles of the lands were divided into smaller parts and were sold on something similar to a free market. However, the people who had the money to buy the deeds were former aristocrats or merchants who had managed to survive throughout the revolution. The class of peasants was still not able to escape from the farming life created thousands of years before.

The industrial revolution served as a curving point for the class of farmers and is viewed by many experts as one of the great equalizers in our history that can be matched only by the creation of firearms. Even though the effect of this industrial revolution can be seen as neither negative nor positive, they can be viewed as either depending on the application.

For instance, the application of machines to aid manual labor set many peasants free of various tasks and allowed those few who were the privileged ones time for specialization and education into different fields of labor paved by the introduction of machines to the industry. However, cabinetmakers, seamstresses, and cobblers saw their once valuable at skills to be rendered obsolete and for this reason, they had to return to farming or to the coal mines in order to make a living.

Those from the lower classes that managed to climb to the upper classes were sensible enough to the low-classes and lead them a hand into finding housing for laborers as well as products that were aimed at them. The classes at the time were blue collar, middle class, and white collar as well as some others. The higher classes owned cars, houses, and later radios and televisions.

Mortgages are not the invention of a particular country. They existed long enough as a loan provided only to those of noble ancestry. After the industrial revolution took place, banks were open to providing mortgage loans of a higher risk to common people due to the increase of wealth over the world. This situation helped the people to have their own homes and if they wanted they could become landlords. Despite the fact that it took thousands of years for people to own their home, it was then opened to many. It has even reached a point where people were able to buy too many properties. However, the problem with mortgages is that accumulating too much debt could make someone lose a house the same way it would help him or her own one.

After this brief history of real estate investing, the bottom line is that land ownership was the factor that helped us have all the investment opportunities we can see today. Land ownership has changed from being earned by strength to something you are able to buy, trade, sell, as well as rent. There always has been a situation where a fee was paid to the owner of land for its exploitation and protection. This tenancy was first offered to tribal leaders, then it was paid to kings, and at the end to landlords.

In the first chapter of this book, we will analyze the different types of real estate investments to help you understand the basics of this business as well as the pros and cons of investing in each one. In the second chapter, we will present you with some key rules of real estate investing as well as the different strategies you can follow in order for you to achieve the goals you have set when you decided to follow this path. In the third chapter, we will analyze the various and most important risks involved when you decide to invest in real estate. This way you will be able to prepare better to avoid or handle the consequences of those risks. In the fourth chapter, we will present how you will be able to start a real estate business and become a successful real estate investor from scratch. Many are afraid to make the leap and make the important decision of investing in real estate. Is it, however, as difficult as everyone thinks?

Real estate investing is an amazing journey filled with challenges and immense profits you should never give up once you start. Let us see the different reasons why this is true throughout the course of this book.

Chapter 1: The Different Types of Real Estate Investments

As we have already established, real estate investing has to do with buying, owning, managing, renting or selling land as well as any structure on it for profit. For many people, investing in real estate has been deemed as uncharted territory. Investing in bonds and stocks, commonly called traditional assets, real estate investments are believed to be an alternative asset that is difficult to afford and access.

Even though this may be true, there is no reason to avoid investing in real estate just because you are not familiar with the way it works as an investment opportunity. When you have a solid investment plan, real estate can be profitable as well as a dependable way for you to multiply your money both in the short and the long term. When done correctly, real estate investing will be able to provide you with a consistent income stream, portfolio diversification, and appreciation potential. However, when someone does not know where to start, real estate investing can seem like a herculean task.

To start with, there are four categories of real estate you can invest in. Those are the following:

- ✓ Residential Real Estate
- ✓ Commercial Real Estate
- ✓ Industrial Real Estate
- ✓ Land

When it comes to residential real estate we usually include single-family homes, condominiums, townhouses, and multi-family homes. There are different types of regulations and laws that define residential real estate when compared to commercial real estate. In real estate, residential property refers to structures that have been zoned or developed for living as the examples we provided previously with the addition of mobile home parks and apartments. Any property that is properly constructed for occupation and for a non-business purpose can be deemed as residential property. In this chapter, we will focus on residential real estate due to the fact that it is the most common investing option for people who want to make their first steps in real estate investing. Below is a list with the structures included in this type of real estate:

- ✓ **Condominiums**: They are privately owned units included within larger communities or buildings. They are similar in structure to this of the apartment buildings. When a person buys a condo, he or she owns the individual unit and all the other unit owners will share joint ownership of all the common areas which are controlled by the management.

- ✓ **Townhomes**: Those are units that are often larger than condos and still have walls with the other buildings.
- ✓ **Cooperatives**: They are units included in one building where the people who live in the building own the structure together.
- ✓ **Single-family houses**: They are commonly constructed on a single lot and do not share space with others living in the area.
- ✓ **Multi-family houses**: Their size often varies from two to four units. For example, you can imagine a duplex or a four-plex. However, anything that is bigger than four units is commercial property.

Apartments are considered as residential property only if they less than five units. Also, camps, hotels, and other places that are used only temporarily by people are not considered residential property. Those types are more efficiently categorized as commercial real estate.

Condominiums

When you use condos as an investment property, you could opt for renting it out to tenants. This way, condos will work as an apartment does. The difference here is that a person can own a different condo, but apartments are rented by someone who claims ownership of the whole building. If you want to buy a condo, you will have to pay a monthly condo fee along with the money you paid to purchase the condo. This monthly fee will cover the upkeep and maintenance of the areas that are shared with the various other owners in the condo community.

So, should you purchase a condo as a way of investing in real estate? Let us see the positive aspects of investing in condos. One of the most important benefits of owning a condo is that others will have to deal with the maintenance of the property's exterior and not you or the tenant thus you will have fewer worries about its maintenance. Neither you nor the tenant will be responsible to mow the lawn or shovel the snow for example. Another benefit of owning a condo is that you will not have to worry about including in your budget expenses such as replacing a roof which can cost a great amount of money. This is the case because you will own only the space that is inside the condo and not the exterior of the structure. The only thing you will have to worry about is the maintenance of the systems and appliances within the unit you own.

Usually, the condo association is responsible for taking care of the troubles and expenses that have to do with the maintenance of the building as well as the grounds. However, each condo association decides which are theirs and the owner's responsibilities. So you will have to read carefully every document the condo association offers you before you make any purchase.

Typically, it is less expensive to buy a condo than for instance a townhouse or a single-family home that has similar features, as an investment. As a result, you will be required to pay less pocket cash. You should make sure that the monthly rent you are charging is able to cover any ownership costs you have such as the fee you have to pay every month for the condo. The purchase of a combo may seem cheaper than that of other real estate investments because there are recurring fees.

Another benefit of investing in condos is the inclusion of high-quality community conveniences such as a club room, fitness room, and a pool. Those amenities can attract many tenants and thus you will be able to keep the unit you own rented with no delays that could cost you money. Keep in mind that properties who include such alluring amenities will usually be high in demand. In other words, if a tenant moves out of your unit, you will be able to have very short vacancies and those are an investor's dream when it comes to maintaining the cash flow.

One more thing that makes condos a reliable real estate investment is the increased security of most condo buildings. Most commonly, you will need a key to enter the building before you are able to get at the front door of your unit. Then, each of the units is equipped with intercom which residents can use and allow in visitors or guests they approve of. This extra security will make any tenant feel very safe, something they will wish to pay for generously in order to enjoy.

Also, there are more rules you will need to abide by when you own a unit in a condo community. For instance, you will need the permission of the condo association to make any alterations to your unit whether it is inside or outside of it. Most probably you will not be able to make any changes to the color of your front door and residents are usually forbidden to keep a home office and conduct businesses. It is a fact that the rules of a condo community are more strict than other similar properties which are not called a condo, however, these rules offer the necessary protection for the units to not be depreciated by preventing unwelcome activities.

The regulations and rules of a condo association are often proven to be exactly what is needed for the existence of a community that will benefit all owners. For example, your tenant will not be able to grow anything he or she likes on the patio, but he will not have to worry about his neighbor's garden turning into a junkyard. You can think of the condo association as a police force that keeps residents from bad behaviors, neglecting and damaging the property and thus maintain the value of the unit.

Moving on to the cons of investing in a condo, the first one is very common for many people. Neighbors, whose behavior is not ideal. Admittedly, you will have neighbors in any community you decide to live in whether they are beside you, above you, or below you. In all the time you will own a condo, there are high chances that your tenant will have a neighbor you wished had never moved in.

This poses a problem because when your neighbors are not welcomed, you will have a hard time to keep your tenant happy. When your tenant is not happy, this may result in higher vacancies than you'd like and a constant search for tenants. Also, since you are the owner, you will have to handle personally on various times any complaints with those neighbors, something that can be very frustrating.

Another drawback of investing in condos is the fact that condo fees will most probably be raised every few years due to inflation. Added to the monthly fees, you may also get a pretty expensive "special assessment." This assessment is an added fee given to each owner for special projects, such as paving all over again the parking lot. If you have not taken any budget measures for such fees, you could end up in a position where you will no longer be able to afford the special assessments or condo fees.

There is also the danger of financial mismanagement by the condo association to think of. The association board that rules the condos often includes condo owners of the community who are elected or volunteer for the position. Usually, the condo buildings are owned by a group of investors who hire a property management company to take care of the collection of the condo fees as well as take care of the management of the community. The governments of each state request from the condos to create and follow legal documents such as articles of incorporation and bylaws.

However, there is still a chance that the condo association could become insolvent or even mismanage funds.

Another drawback that has to do with the condo association can be the poor management of properties. For instance, if a condo association is not doing its job well when it comes to maintaining the common areas, it can cause damage to the entire community. Since you are an owner, you will rely on the association to follow through their end of the bargain and do anything to maintain the value of your property. Their inability to manage the properties properly and make the needed upgrades to the building and to the community will affect the long-term appreciation of your property, making you lose quality tenants that would want to rent your unit.

As we have mentioned before, condo communities have rules that could both restrict and protect you. When it comes to limiting your freedom, condo rules can prevent you from renting out your unit. For example, most of the condo communities have a limit on the units that can be rented. If a tenant moves out, someone else rents another unit, and this limit is reached, you will not be able to rent your unit.

Another thing the condo association may limit is the length of the lease, the number of occupants, and various others that have to do with how you will be able to use your condo.

With these policies, they aim for the prevention of turning the property into an apartment building rather than a community where owners reside. For you to be safe, you will have to make sure you will be able to rent your unit before you buy it and also secure that your tenants will be able to abide by the condo requirements. You can learn much information about the condo association from other tenants that live in a condo community. Ask them how it is like living there.

Townhouses

We can trace the origins of the modern townhouse back to early England when this term was linked to a property that a person had "in town". This type of real estate was usually owned by royalty or nobility since their main residence would normally be in the country. This term was maintained today and is used to include a wide range of residences and not as a home for only the wealthy. A townhouse is a single-family home that should share a wall with another house and have at least two floors. Each townhome is owned independently unlike a duplex or a fourplex and as the owner you will be able to rent it to others. Let us delve deeper into the pros and cons of owning a townhouse or else a townhome.

To start with, if you want to invest in a townhouse and later rent it or sell it, it is considered to be an affordable option when it comes to housing for families. After a quick research, you will discover that townhouses will be more popular in areas where the prices of buying or renting property are high and there are only little options of available land. There are places in the United States for example, where you will not see townhouses at all and you will see somewhere land is available.

Another benefit of investing in a townhouse is that you will be able to own the interior as well as the exterior of the building in contrast with investing in a condo. Even though townhouses are similar to condominiums, their main difference is that you own the exterior of the house. As we have analyzed, in condos, you will only own the interior of your unit.

There may be rules to follow which are determined by Homeowners Association as well as some added expenses to support the association, but its existence will be an added bonus for you to make sure that the value of your property will remain at high levels. Also, when your neighbors neglect to take care of their own property, Homeowners Association will be able to enforce certain rules that could include a foreclosure if they fail to comply. The expenses may be higher due to the association, but you will not see much difference from owning a single-family home with similar rules.

Added to the above benefits, you will be able to make your own decisions concerning your property. This is not true when it comes to owning a condominium, where stiff rules exist when it comes to the decisions you will be able to make for your property. For instance, when you own a condo, not being able to make decisions about the exterior of your home can be a considerable restriction for you and your tenant. Any replacement, upgrades, or maintenance work will be straight from the condo association and the bill will be sent straight to you for changes that were not yours. With townhouses, you will fully own the property and thus making the important decisions will be your responsibility concerning the necessary upgrades.

As for all maintenance expenses, when you own a townhouse you will not have to take them up completely on your own. With a single-family house, you will be totally alone when it comes to all the maintenance responsibilities, everything will have to go through your budget. Townhouses offer you a more lenient budget since there are some opportunities for you to save up costs. This is the case because you will be sharing one or two walls with your neighbors and thus there will be fewer expenses to consider. When you own a townhouse, your tenant will still be a part of a big community but without the restrictions of the condo association.

Due to the fact that more common areas with townhouse communities tend to be more available compared to other communities, you and your tenant will also be able to enjoy the benefits of having near a picnic area, an open space, and a playground, but keep in mind that those areas are shared within the community.

Also, you should consider the fact that townhouses tend to be faster to sell than other homes. When you invest in a townhouse, you are purchasing a property that will target two groups of potential buyers: families who wish to downsize and first-time owners. This translates to you being able to sell the property faster than you would if you owned a different unit. If you want to up the value of the townhome you purchase and later want to sell or rent, you could spend some time and money to soundproof your unit so as to avoid hearing any noise from the neighbors.

Since you will be living in a community, there will be common areas that will be accessible by everyone living there such as gardens, a small park, a lawn, or a playground under the responsibility of the association. However, if the townhouse has a back or front yard, it will be your or your tenant's responsibility to maintain it as well as the exterior of the house. But if your tenant likes to do work outside, mow the lawn, or create your own landscaping, this could be a problem for him or her. Most of the families living in townhouses prefer to have other people take care of these things for them since it allows them to spend more time with their families.

A townhouse will benefit greatly families, who lead a hectic lifestyle. For instance, new families will have multiple responsibilities varying from going back and forth to work, taking the kids to school and extracurricular activities, running errands, and struggling to find some family quality time to spend with each other. If you were to invest and rent a single-family house, your tenant would have to take out of his or her precious extra time to deal with the exterior chores. This problem will be solved by owning and renting out a townhouse.

Security is another benefit to consider when investing in a townhome. If your tenant or buyer needs to travel often due to the nature of his work or for family matters, then his house will not be left in the hands of burglars. For instance, single-family homes will require the tenant to hire someone to clean the pool or maw the lawn while he or she is away.

Also, the privacy of single-family homes can be seen as an invitation to burglars. When you or your tenant pays the fees of the association, then security is can be included in the benefits of investing in a townhome. When someone sees unknown people lurking around, they will take action to protect your property. Besides security, this could also apply to other things such as noticing a leaking roof faster or other maintenance related issues.

Finally, another benefit could be that most townhomes will allow your tenant to be closer to town. When it comes to single-family homes, they may be in a secluded area well into the country. Townhomes are most commonly found in the city or in the suburbs. This means that it will be easier to find a tenant because he or she will be closer to his or her work, near restaurants as well as other entertainment options and public transportation to lessen vehicle expenses.

Moving on to the disadvantages of investing in a townhome, the first one would be that townhouses are closely related to an apartment or a condo than a single-family home. This translates to seeing and hearing, especially if your walls are thin, your neighbors more often within this community. Even though the nature of townhomes can help you, your tenant or buyer be a part of a supportive and friendly community, the possibilities of having to deal with households that are not very friendly or concerned with maintaining the environment and their home clean are high.

Since you will own the townhouse for a while, this could affect the overall value of your property when you will wish to rent or sell it. To deal with this problem, you should first ask around and make a profile of the community the property you wish to buy is a part of.

When compared to a detached single-family home, the sense of privacy in a townhouse will be limited. This is a factor you tenant or buyer will have to consider. Another factor to consider is the sense of ownership in case you intend to sell or rent the property. Even though your buyer or tenant will have fewer maintenance chores to worry about, the fees paid to the association in order for them to maintain the common structures and areas may be high and in the long run your tenant or buyer will have to choose a single-family home to purchase or rent.

You will also have to pay monthly maintenance fees to the association and this happens for all townhomes and condos upon signing. The fee you may not expect is the one called the "capital contribution fee." This extra expense is paid at the transfer or the closing of the townhouse title. The amount varies and is based on the agreement, but it can usually be three times the monthly maintenance charge. The amount is assessed and consistent with the bylaws of the association your property belongs to. If this expense is not included in the MLS listing of your contract, you should ask about it before agreeing to purchase or sign anything binding.

Due to the fact that townhouses are commonly built in places of premium land, they usually stretch upward to have more space available. You may see a three-story or four-story unit with only one or two rooms on each floor. Such a design requires the usage of stairs often and thus it can pose a challenge for people who suffer from physical limitations. This option can be impractical for instance for families who have young children, people with disabilities, and the elderly. This problem can be solved if you talk before your purchase with the people living there and install an elevator system, however, keep in mind that there may not be enough room for you to do so.

From an investor's point, this could mean a loss of potential tenants or buyers since people will not be able to grow old in this home, for example. In other words, keep in mind that this is not always a solid investment when compared to a single-family home.

Another disadvantage can be the fact that townhouses do not appreciate fast when compared to other options you have in real estate. Even though you will find some exceptions to this rule, the norm is that most townhomes will not appreciate in value at the same pace a single-family home will. Also, if there is a housing bubble in the community you wish to make your investment at, the value will depreciate slower, but it cannot be considered as an investment where you will be able to make a lot of cash.

Added to the above disadvantages, you may have to respond to the complaints of neighbors as the owner about things that may be trivial, especially if you are renting this property you may also have to listen to your tenant complain about the neighbors. If you or your tenant fails to respond to complaints such as food smell, for instance, a lien will be placed on your home and thus you will b forced to make time to respond to complaints, even the ridiculous ones.

One last disadvantage of townhouses is the limited available storage options. For example, if your tenant or buyer wishes to fully decorate the property for each holiday or has kids with lots of toys and needs space for that entire plus two or three bicycles, a townhouse will not have, most times, the necessary storage or closet room for those things. You will need to have an offer prepared for an additional storage unit to satisfy the needs of your clients. In contrast, a single-family home will offer that additional storage room in the form of basement areas, a garage, and attic space. Townhomes usually will not even offer outdoor space for someone to store children's toys or stuff for your pet, things that larger families will typically need.

Cooperative Buildings

Moving on to the next type of residential type of property, cooperative buildings or else "co-ops" are defined as a unique form of housing option that can be found in limited numbers to the United States urban markets. Those forms of housing option first appeared in the United States in the late

1800s and rose in popularity in Washington DC in the 1920s. Nowadays cooperative buildings are very popular in Chicago.

To better understand the nature of a cooperative building, it is a property including many units that are owned by a company, most commonly a Limited-Liability Company (LLC). People who buy a unit in this building will turn into shareholders of the company that controls the property and attain exclusive leasehold of the unit they purchase. This means that the unit you will buy will be financed in the form of a home loan and not in the form of a residential mortgage since you will be buying shares in a company and not a real property.

The property that the company owns is managed by a cooperative building board consisting of a limited number of the shareholders, who are entrusted with making decisions that will benefit the corporation and thus other residents. This arrangement is different from a legal perspective than the one we analyzed with condos since, in the case of the condos; each unit has an individual owner. The board of the cooperative building will get involved in all the purchases as well as sales by reviewing and approving all the applicants. Let us see the advantages and disadvantages of this arrangement.

In some cases, an advantage of this form of housing is the fact that cooperative buildings sometimes can be a less expensive option for housing. You will find them usually cheaper, in terms of per square foot than, for example, condos in the same area. Keep in mind that they also have low closing costs. When it comes to being in a high-cost housing market, cooperative buildings can be a long-term investment since a future sale of your unit can have as a result, important financial gains, despite the fact that the future owners will not be building equity.

When it comes to the disadvantages, owners will be able to not pay attention to chores relating to property management outside their units, but they will still have to pay a considerable amount of these expenses and due to the nature of ownership, the cost may be high. Also, when it comes to taxes, cooperative building owners will have to deal with different tax rules than homeowners who have mortgages. In the second group, those people will most commonly enjoy tax deductions. Added to this, if the board passes a major project for changes in the units, you will have to pay your part in it, even if you did not agree to the changes. Your part in these costs may be substantial.

When it comes to owning a unit in cooperative buildings, the board will have to approve of any new tenant and this includes the possibility of a new roommate. So, if you need to rent your unit, the new resident must be informed of those circumstances. As far as renovations are concerned, you may also need the approval of the board to make any changes to your unit. The approval for this may take a long time and it will most probably include an application fee. Another disadvantage can be the fact that you may not be able to rent your unit for a short time and if a tenant is not approved by the board, you will not be able to rent at all, even if you approve of him or her.

In addition to the above, if you are allowed to rent your unit, there are various co-ops that allow only a limited percentage of the unit to be leased and they may also ask for minimum residency that can typically be for up to three years before you will be able to make an approval application. When it comes to the approval of residents, in the United States cooperative boards must do so based on the Fair Housing Act. This act forbids discrimination based on national origin, sex, race, family status, religion, and disability. Those classes are protected by the government and states may have added classes based on marital status, height, source of income or sexual orientation.

Single Family Homes

Moving on, we will see the different benefits and drawbacks of investing in a single-family home. A single-family detached home is a structure in which one family is living and this structure is not attached to another building. Let us start by presenting the benefits of this investing choice.

The first benefit we could present to you is that tenants, in case of renting, will lease for longer than in the other cases of property investment. There are many single-family properties that are rented for one year and longer which is longer when compared to apartments or condos. Most families, who seek to rent a single-family home, usually want to save up and buy a new one. Keep in mind that the longer the leases last; they will increase the annual Return of Investment for you.

Another benefit of investing in a single-family home is that it holds its resale value, especially if it is maintained well and its location is ideal, for instance, in a thriving and well-reputed neighborhood. If those two requirements are met, your investment will almost certainly hold higher resale value. This is not true for neighborhoods that suffer from crime and declining economy since it will lose its value very quickly.

Also, detached single-family homes have lower annual property taxes when compared to multi-family homes or apartment buildings. Added to this, commercial real estate can be often taxed differently and taxes may be higher when compared to single-family homes. When it comes to costs, another benefit can be that single-family homes have lower management costs due to the fact that small families live inside. This is true especially when you have a tenant who will take excellent care of the house and thus lessen the costs of repairs that fall upon you with the renewal of each lease.

When it comes to the cons of investing in a single-family home, you should keep in mind that unlike multi-family homes, single-family homes are most commonly vacant the moment the lease ends. For this reason, you may have to budget for repairs after a vacancy, you will lose revenue from the times it stays vacant and your costs will be increased for finding a new tenant. Also, in most neighborhoods, the common property for an average single-family home is less than ¼ acre. Typically, families opt for renting a property with more land for convenience and this fact can translate into taking more time to find a new tenant to rent.

Last but not least, we have listed as a benefit the fact that single-family homes typically hold their resale value no matter how long before the property was constructed. This can be seen as a drawback too since the initial price of your investment will be high. When those homes are renovated before they are placed on the market, they will have a higher price for sale when compared to those that will need extra work for repairs during the time you will buy them.

Multi-Family Homes

The last type of residential property we are going to analyze is the multi-family home. Multi-family homes are properties designed to meet the needs and accommodate many families in various units inside the house. You will see these properties in many forms such as duplexes or triplexes as well as apartment buildings that can be considered multi-family homes. Many people consider them an investment choice but through the following analysis of pros and cons, you will be able to form a better opinion on whether this is the right investment for you.

One of the benefits of investing in multi-family homes is the number of money you will get by renting this property. By hosting many families in one property, your cash flow will increase, given the fact that each family will pay their part over the maintenance and ownership of the property. Each of the families living there will be a boost to your income, thus making single-family homes less profitable than the multi ones.

In terms of simplicity and convenience, a multi-family home will offer you the chance to deal with on mortgage instead of multiple ones that would be necessary to own multiple single-family homes. If you buy, for instance, a duplex with one mortgage you will have to deal with less paperwork and you will save more time than investing in more single-family homes. The same goes for insurance policies. When you own a multi-family home, you will have to deal with one insurance policy, even though it will be more expensive, you will not be open to multiple and different policies.

If you decide to invest in a multi-family home, you will mitigate your risk of being without tenants for a considerable amount of time and losing revenue. This is true because you will be dealing with three or more units, so the risk of a complete vacancy is not high. Even if you have one family move out, you will have other tenants to keep your revenues coming and maintain a positive level as you wait to fill the empty unit. Also, if the tenant of one unit delays in paying the rent, the other tenants can make up for the lost time.

Also, the competition for renting and purchasing single-family homes is considerably high because it is considered to be an easy way to enter the area of real estate investing. For this reason, if you choose to invest in multi-family homes, you will have less competition in terms of biding for rent and purchases. Added to this, the price of single-family homes is most commonly based on which house families find appealing, which is often based on different neighborhoods and the changes within them. On the other hand, multi-family homes are priced based on the potential they have to generate income for the investor. They are considered primarily as a form of investment and for this reason, they are bought and sold, so they have more stable growth in the long term.

Moving on to the downsides of investing in a multi-family property, the first one would be the price they are sold at. They are more expensive than single-family homes. Even though you will not be required to pay for a double price when it comes to a duplex one, if you aim to invest in homes with more than three units, prices can be very high. If you are low on cash and this is your first investment in properties, multi-family homes may be too expensive for you to consider.

Also, by owning a multi-family property, you will need to make room for more management time since each unit in the house will result in more responsibilities when it comes to management and more time to be spent for you taking up the role of a landlord. You will have to deal with many tenants at the same time, different sets of appliances, and different schedules. Not to mention that if something breaks in the property it will affect many other units at once and thus making the repair bills larger.

When we analyzed the pros of investing in a multi-family property, we mentioned that you will have fewer competitors to deal with when compared to single-family properties. However, the type of competition will change. Due to the advantages and nature of multi-family property investing, these units tend to be the targets of experienced investors with many more years of experience on their backs than you have. This can result in you finding difficult searching for tenants as well as pricing your units the right way.

Another thing you should keep in mind is that multi-family properties are typically more complicated than single-family homes. For example, if you end up with a tenant that causes trouble, all the other tenants are going to suffer from it or if you end up with a structural damage, the price of your property will fall considerably. Also, multi-family homes are not that freely available, including those who are lower in demand, than single-family homes. This translates to you facing some difficulties finding the perfect property for your needs since your options will be limited.

One last drawback of multi-family homes is that you will have to research the various regulations about how you will be able t rent your property. This includes the laws of your state so as to not risk imprisonment or paying fines for not abiding by the rules. Keep in mind that rules for multi-family homes are stricter than those who govern single-family properties. Even though multi-family homes can be very profitable, they are also very challenging and complicated.

Now that we have seen the various residential properties you can invest in, let us see the different investment strategies you can apply to your investing career and make reliable as well as profitable choices.

Chapter 2: The Real Estate Investing Strategies

It is true that the real estate market can be deemed as intimidating by some people. However, it is not a faraway dream for people and like everything else you need to know a few things before you get yourself involved. For instance, the golden rule of real estate investment is location. Location is the first thing to consider when you want to choose a property to invest in.

For example, college towns demand rental property. Even though, in this case, you might be afraid to rent your property at a crazy college kid that will make more harm than good, there are many professors or graduate students as well as support staff that will need to rent a house in a college town. To be on the safe side you could protect your real estate investment, in such a case, with checking your potential tenant's financial statements, references, or credit checks.

You could also try to invest in a property that is close to the area you are living, let us say thirty minutes from where your house. This has some appeal since you will know the area well and you will be able to respond quickly to problems that have to do with your property instead of hiring someone to do it for you. However, there are also some disadvantages that have to do with the fact that you may not be able to afford to invest in property of your local area or that you may not be able to purchase as many properties as you would like given the prices. Also, if your area gets hit by an economic slump or a natural disaster occurs, your properties will be vulnerable since they will all be around the same place.

When you are searching for properties to buy, there are various aspects you have to think of apart from the economic picture of the area you are searching at. For example, is this area visited or filled with younger people? Young people are more likely to rent than older people since they move around more. They want to live in central places, preferably in cities with lots of events, a certain culture, a good bar, and a good restaurant. Also, a considerable percentage of people do not own cars, so they will choose to live in cities that are friendly to bicycles, are walkable, and have an easy transportation system. Apart from that, you should also check the crime rate of the area you wish to invest in. No one will want to live in a neighborhood where crime is an everyday occurrence. In order for you to be certain about such things, you could read the local newspapers, ask around or look at a crime map.

Another factor to consider when you wish to enter the real estate market is how much money you are able to spend. The answer to this part will depend greatly on whether you are able to pay with cash if you have to take a mortgage. For both options, there are benefits and drawbacks to consider.

When you are able to pay with cash, you will be able to avoid the mortgage process and thus you will not have to pay interests. Also, if you are able to make an offering for a property in cash, you may take many steps ahead of your competition since sellers like cash payments. However, if you have a limited amount of cash you are able to invest, paying with this method is not the ideal choice since it will tie your hands in one asset and you will not be diversified.

When it comes to leveraging or else mortgaging, there are several financial sites that recommend this choice as the best one since the investor will be able to have the cash to invest in various assets and achieve diversification. This way you will be able to buy more than one property and you can make sure that your money will be invested in more than one property and be open to possibly different markets if your properties are in different cities.

However, if the real estate market went into a crisis mode and the values of the properties declined sharply, you will be in a position where you are going to owe more money than the house itself is worth. To lessen the risks involved, it would be good if you did your homework beforehand when it comes to the different mortgage terms offered that will best suit you and the properties you wish to invest in.

Another rule that many real estate investors follow is the 1% rule. This simple rule states that the monthly rent of a property should be equal or greater than 1% of the value of the home you purchased in order for you to get the best return of investment. For instance, if you purchased a property for $100.000, your rent should be $1.000 per month. If the amount of rent is less than what your research on other houses in the area has shown, the selling price of the home is probably overpriced. This rule will not tell you everything and you don't have to adhere to it without a thought, but it is a good starting point and a nice way to assess the long list of properties you are assessing as your future real estate investments.

Added to the above, if you are new to the area of real estate investing and you have never owned your own home, you probably are not aware of the various things to look for about the different problems or the things that could cause problems within a home. To solve this problem, you could hire a home inspector who has about 1.600 items on his or her list of things to watch out for, maybe even more.

If your home inspector does find problems, you could start negotiations with the seller to fix the issues the inspector pointed out or to reduce the price of the property so as for you to fix those problems yourself. Keep in mind that the home inspector may find so many problems with the house that you will have to pass on the purchase of this particular property.

For instance, a home inspector may look at the age of the roof; list all the cracks on the home foundations, note the exterior condition, and search for any signs of water damage. For this reason, a home inspection is not the thing to cut off your list if you want to save money. If this step is passed, then you will have to pay double the amount of purchase to make this house livable for others to rent.

Another golden rule of real estate investing is for the investor to have an emergency fund for his or her rental property. This step will not only protect the investment you will make, but it will also keep you at peace. An emergency fund will include money sealed in a savings account to be used for unexpected expenses and routine repairs such as fixing various small damages in between tenants or replacing a roof after a natural disaster occurs.

A common method followed by mortgage lenders is for a buyer to have saved at least 6 months' worth of mortgage payments before the loan is given. However, if the home you want to invest in is older and for this reason, will need more repairs compared to a new property, you will most likely have to increase that amount. That number should also be higher when the history of this property indicates, long times of vacancies between tenants.

There is a lot of work involved in real estate investment and not only for finding the right house to invest in and in the right place that will offer you more revenues. For instance, you have to advertise your property and be able to respond to maintenance problems, deal with cases of eviction and collect the rent, not to mention the construction of the lease. Then, you need to be prepared to make all these things again when a tenant moves out. If you are not able to do all these things by yourself you may have to hire a property management company.

You could also create a team, instead of hiring a property management company, that will help you through this process, especially if you aim to purchase and own more properties than one or two. For you to make the best team is the reputation each person has. Some suggestions of positions that you need to fill for your team are a real estate agent, a property manager, and a home inspector.

To have a better understanding of how you could make money from real estate investing, there are various strategies to consider as a new investor. Think of the process you are going to follow as the mountain that is real estate investing and the careful climber that is you, the investor. In order for you to reach the top, which is your life and financial goals, you will have to go through several sub-goals before you achieve your main one.

Strategies are as useful as the map of a mountain is. They show you the different routes you will have to take in order to reach the peak safely and quickly. Strategies also include tactics that can be viewed as the necessary tools for you to climb to that mountain following the route you chose. However, before you consider which tactics are best, you should get clear on your goal for investing in real estate such as financial freedom, then pick one or two strategies that fit your needs and then get clear on the tactics.

Due to the variety of strategies available for real estate investors, we are going to follow a model where strategies are divided into groups based on the end result they provide. For example, the first group of real estate investing strategies we are going to present, are business strategies. Strategies of real estate investing under the category of business strategies are viewed as a way to develop your own business rather than make some investments. In other words, your investments will grow to generate income that will be able to support all your needs and could replace your job. However, if you choose to follow the strategies included in this group, you must be prepared to invest not only money but a lot of effort and time during your business start-up in order to be successful.

Fix-and-Flip

The first strategy of the business group is the Fix-and-Flip one. According to this strategy, the investor will have to follow a business path of searching for properties that need work including doing all the necessary repairs and then selling them again at a higher price to make a profit. By following this model, your aim will be to make money in order to generate savings for your future investments and pay the bills. Renovating the houses you purchase will not be an easy job, but the later selling price will make all your efforts worth it.

Flipping a property is admittedly a riskier investment than rental properties and as is the case with every risky business the rewards can be immense if all your plans are safely carried out or it could turn into a disaster if your plans fail. One of the benefits of flipping a property is the considerable potential you have to achieve a quick profit. Most investors who opt for real estate flip are hoping to make money faster than in other real estate investing methods. Also, with this method, you will be able to gain experience in various areas that will later help you with building your future in real estate investing.

For instance, you will gain experience and learn more about construction. If you follow real estate flip you will need to take care of the remodeling, the renovation, and repairing of the properties you purchase. This will offer you insight into different areas of construction. You will be able to understand, after a certain point, how much different materials cost as well as the various electrical and plumbing repairs. You will also be able to do to a certain degree the job of a property inspector by spotting big issues each house has on its structure and environment such as asbestos and mold. As you delve deeper and carry out more projects, through this construction experience you will be able to recognize the various ways you could generate more money on future projects since you will know how to seal the best budget deal.

Also, you will learn how to conduct a market research. Always before making a purchase for a house to flip, you should conduct market research to look for the best deals you can make. For example, you could talk to real estate brokers in the area you look to purchase, look for "for sale" advertisements, and search for houses that have been recently sold to get a better idea on the selling prices as well as what people are looking for in a house in that area.

Market research is essential because you have to know your target audience. For example, in one part of a country, people would want a modern house design while in another part; buyers will opt for a more traditional house design. Your renovation goals should be similar to the demand of the market of your choice, otherwise, you will have to sell the renovated house at a lower price or even worse not be able to sell it at all.

You will instantly gain more experience the moment you place the first property you flipped up for sale. This is true because you will have a better insight into the various things buyers are searching for in the are of your first sale. It would be best if you kept notes on what buyers liked or did not like to make the necessary changes in your following projects. Another thing you will learn about this type of property investment with your first flip are the unexpected costs. It would be better for everyone, especially investors if everything went according to plan, however, you'd be surprised at how many times this does not happen.

Every investment has risks and this is why it is necessary to learn how to mitigate risks. This includes the unexpected costs that will come your way. Through experience, you will learn how to plan expenses for contractor disputes, construction delays, building permits, delays in delivery materials, and keeping up with the costs of when you are not able to sell your property as quickly as you had initially planned.

Also, another benefit of this real estate investment strategy is that you will increase your network. Throughout every flipping project, you will make new contacts in the industry such as building inspectors, real estate brokers, other investors, attorneys, insurance brokers, and contractors. These contacts will be useful for any future investment you will make, so try to be at your best behavior and always be professional when you are dealing with such people.

Last but not least, you will feel proud because you will be able to see the potential of a property that others will not be able to. This is an advantage of a real estate flip that can also be developed through experience. You have a vision that can increase the value of a home when others thought it was merely useless and with no value.

On the other hand, there are several disadvantages to consider with this method of real estate investing. The main one is the risk of losing large sums of money instead of making large sums of money. There are various factors that can lead to this worst-case scenario such as:

- ✓ Unexpected costs: Even though you will learn in time how to control the various sources where unexpected costs come from, unanticipated costs such as contractor delays, permit delays, material delays, building permits and renovations you had not planned, can add up very quickly and lead you to make no profits.
- ✓ High taxes: Once the renovations you had planned for your property are complete, the city may choose to increase the taxes you will have to pay for your

property. As a result, you will probably face many difficulties finding a buyer and thus be forced to pay those taxes yourself and even if you find one, the added taxes may make him rethink buying your property.

✓ Other costs: If you have a mortgage on the property, you will have to pay for it even after the renovations are complete. Also, you will have to pay the insurance and taxes on the property for the period of time you will own it. These are costs that will take a large sum out of your budges and the costs will be greater the longer the ownership stays in your hands. Another thing to consider is the maintenance costs since the yard will have to be cleaned, as well as the snow, and the grass will have to be cut.

Selling difficulties: In real estate investing and especially for this strategy, you lose money for each day you cannot find a buyer to sell your property due to the fact that you will have to pay for the costs of holding the property. Also, for the longer, the property remains available in the market, the likelihood of having to reduce the selling price, which will be a hit to your expected profits.

Another drawback of this real estate strategy is the stress associated with it. You will have to find the right property, plan properly for all the costs involved and deal with contractors. Stress is something you will have to learn to control in the long run, but at first, it will be there.

Wholesaling

Another real estate investment strategy is wholesaling. Wholesaling is defined as the business when an investor finds good deals of properties and then resells them almost instantly with a small heightened price. In order for you to be good at this business you have to develop negotiating and marketing skills in order to be able to fish those good deals. For this business, you also have to like sales and be good at them. If this is true then you will be good at wholesaling. However, if you hate sales, you must choose a different real estate investment strategy.

This type of strategy is one of the perfect choices for investors who want to make profits from short-term investments. The process that is usually followed is:

- ✓ Finding a property for sale
- ✓ Having the property for sale under contract

✓ Selling the property to another investor

Due to the fact that a wholesale real estate investor does not keep the properties, he or she invests in or holds them for using them as rental properties, wholesaling in real estate is deemed as short-term investments. Let us see the steps to be followed in wholesaling real estate.

In the wholesale real estate investment strategy, the first step is to find a property up for sale. Keep in mind that not any property that is up for sale will be ideal for a wholesale investor. The properties that will do the job will be priced below market value or have motivated sellers, as is called in the real estate world. Motivated sellers are the ones who are willing to sell a real estate investment at a lower price. Let us see the different ways you will be able to find such a property for sale that fits the wholesaling real estate definition:

✓ With comparative market analysis: It will determine if the property is sold below market value.
✓ By developing a real estate network to discover motivated sellers.
✓ With indulging in real estate investment marketing.

Through a visit to the city hall of the area you want to invest in. There, you will find a list of properties available in the real estate market that are believed to be fixer-upper investment properties or are near to foreclosure.

The next step to this strategy is to place the property for sale under contract. Once you find the appropriate property for sale, which is below market value or you negotiated with a motivated seller for a reduced price, you will have to pay for a wholesale real estate contract. This will cost you approximately $10.

The last step of this investment strategy is for you to sell the property to another real estate investor. It would be wise for you to already have searched and find the real estate investor before you even make the offer for the property that is for sale. This way, you will have a guarantee that your property will be sold quickly. A common practice amongst real estate investors is to buy low and sell high. However, this is not the case for a wholesale investor who buys low and also sells the property for a low price. This happens because the new buyer must have a good return on his or her investment.

Let us see an example to better understand this strategy. If you, as a wholesaler, find a property that is worth $150.000 after the necessary repairs are made, you managed to negotiate the price down to $125.000. So, a good price for this property, after the contract is made, will be $140.000. This way, the wholesale investor will profit and the buyer will be able to make a good return of investment after he or she makes additional repairs.

The above is the most basic form of wholesaling in real estate. You are probably able to understand the pros and cons of the above analysis, but let us delve deeper into them. To start with, one of the main benefits of this investing model is that it does not require a cash investment. You will have no down payments, no credit score review, and no monthly mortgage payments.

Another benefit will be that this way is the faster path to make money through real estate investing. This is one of the reasons why many investors of this field chose wholesaling real estate because they are able to make quick money from it. If you manage to find properties that are sold below market value, you will be able to sell it quickly to a real estate investor due to the positive return of investment you are able to bring on the table.

Even though it may take you some time to discover properties for sale with such requirements as well as the real estate investors to buy them, you will typically be done with a property in a matter of a few months. You will probably be wondering why wholesaling is considered one of the fastest methods to make money in real estate and the answer will be because you will not have to wait for rental income, checks, and for all the renovations to be over.

Wholesaling is also recommended for beginners in real estate investing because there is no cash investment involved and not much experience is needed for you to follow this strategy. Also, through research and good planning, there is little risk involved, something that helps beginners move forward in this field of investing. Wholesaling real estate can be a great opportunity to learn all you need to know about real estate investing in a relatively safe manner. You will be able to develop necessary skills such as negotiating the price of a property, to find properties that are sold below market value and recognize the specific points of a good deal. Added to this, you will be able to create a good real estate network through this method that will later help you if you wish to switch strategies.

An important benefit we briefly mentioned before is the low risk involved in such an investment. Investments that are low on risks are always chaced by real estate investors because it is not as easy as many would think to find low-risk investments in the real estate market. Beginners should always watch out for investment opportunities and grasp every chance they can get their hands on to make a good deal through negotiation. In other words, wholesaling is considered to be a low-risk investment because the amount of cash that is at stake is not that much when compared to the losses of other real estate investment strategies.

Moving on to the drawbacks of wholesale real estate investing the first one would be that there is no guarantee on regular income. This means that there are high chances of wholesale real estate investing not being able to replace your full-time job since once the property is purchased, it will not make you any more money. On the other hand, rental properties will benefit you in having a stable income that real estate investors will be able to rely on.

Also, the fact that wholesale real estate investments are considered to be an easy and quick way of making money in this field, it does not mean that you will not have to dedicate a considerable amount of effort. Until you gain the necessary experience of finding properties priced below market value as well as the investors that wish to buy from you, those steps can cause you a lot of trouble and effort in wholesaling real estate investing. Networking is essential and it cannot be done in a matter of a few days.

You need to be dedicated and learn everything you can lay your hands on finding the appropriate properties for investing, the right sellers that are willing to reduce the price of the property you are interested in as well as the right buyers. Once you have learned how wholesaling real estate investing works, you will be a successful real estate investor.

The following three strategies we are going to present are considered to be the safest when someone wants to start in real estate investing and there are even some cases where little work is required as well as a considerably small amount of cash. Let us see those strategies in more detail.

House Hacking

When the term house hacking is used, it refers to someone who lives in a home that can produce income for this person. Such houses can be a triplex, duplex, fourplex, and generally houses that have extra space which can be rented like spare bedrooms, guest house, or a basement. It is considered to be another great way to invest in real estate because by renting your extra space, you will be able to reduce your housing costs. For instance, you can rent your space to a person that will, in turn, pay off your mortgage. This strategy is different than other traditional ways of investing in real estate because you are living in the property you invest in.

An example of house hacking can be the following. You can buy a four-unit property and reside in one of the four units. Then, you will be able to rent the other three in order to cover your monthly mortgage costs. This property is considered to be occupied by the owner due to the fact that you are living in one of the units. For this reason, you will be able to be financed through mortgages easier, but the interest rate may be a bit increased due to the risk of owning a property with many units.

Continuing with our example, let us assume that your fees per month for housing are $2.000, if you are able to rent the three remaining units for $750 per month, your monthly rent will reach in total $2.250. To translate the numbers, with $2.250 you will be covering your monthly fees and then have $150 leftover for your needs. This is an example of how house hacking works.

You will still have to pay for the upkeep and the maintenance of the property as well as for the times the other units or rooms stay vacant if tenants move out or if they refuse to pay. This is the risk of house hacking. You will have no guarantee that your tenants will pay and you are going to make a profit out of renting your spare space. This could result in your inability to pay your monthly mortgage. However, if it does work you will be able to make money monthly and live for free without having to worry about making ends meet to pay your mortgage.

Now that we have explained better how house hacking works, let us take a better look at the pros and cons of this real estate investment strategy. The obvious benefit we stressed before is that you will have an extra income to pay your mortgage each month instead of having to pay it on your own. Also, you will have reduced housing expenses, since the person you are letting live in your extra space will have to contribute to the house bills every month. This can be applied to utilities such as phone, cable, water, gas, internet, electric, etc. You will split those bills evenly for the other tenants to pay too.

The main drawback of house hacking as a real estate investment is that your home is not really yours. If you are residing in a property with many units, you will be able to place some space between you and your tenants. However, if you have a single-family house, you will share many rooms with those you are renting your space to and that could result in various awkward and even annoying situations. Also, things could get serious if they fail to pay their rent on time or if they want you to do them a "favor". Not to mention the danger of your tenants damaging your units.

To sum up, here is a list of the various ways you can follow the house hack strategy for real estate investing:

- ✓ Purchase a multi-unit property and reside in the units that are not for rent.
- ✓ Rent an empty room at your single-family house.
- ✓ Reside in the guesthouse and rent your main home.
- ✓ Rent all of the rooms of your house and live in the garage or sleep on the couch.
- ✓ Place your house for rent through Airbnb.

Live-In Home Flipping

The live-in home flipping strategy has to do with you buying and living into a house, making the necessary renovations to fix it up and wait for approximately two years or more to sell it and make a profit. You can buy one of the ugliest homes that are located in some of the best neighborhoods and spend the next few years to fix it up. By waiting two years to resell it, you will get out of paying considerable amounts of cash in taxes for the profit. For instance, an individual would reach up to $250.000 and for a couple of $500.000.

The above is one of the most obvious benefits of live-in house flipping. You will be exempt from having to pay capital gain taxes on the sale of the property if you have resided in the house for at least two out of five years. With this real estate investing strategy, you will not have to buy a property and then sell it very fast. For this reason, you will not have to acquire two mortgages since you can take your time to sell the home.

Given the time you will have to reside in the home you will later sell, you can save up money from construction if you do some of the work yourself. If you know a thing or two about fixing a house, you will be able to buy a house that is not in the best condition since they are cheaper than relatively newly constructed ones. However, do some research on this matter because some locales require you to hire a professional. There are many cases of people who followed this real estate investing strategy and had to budget only for raw materials to renovate the house.

Another benefit of this strategy is that you will be able to use an owner-occupied mortgage financing. As an investor, you will have to place at least 20% down for an investment home mortgage with probably higher interest rates. This is not the case with owner-occupied mortgages.

One of the drawbacks of this strategy is that you will have to move around a lot if you want to make considerable profits that are tax-free. Your home will also turn into a construction zone. So, if you have a thing for extreme cleanliness and can't bear the thought of having dust lying in your house, this is not the real estate investing strategy for you. Also, if you are used to having many people over you house for entertainment purposes, you will have to stop or lessen the visits considerably. Another thing you have to keep in mind is that you may have to get used to having workers around the house all the time. They may use inappropriate language you don't want your children to hear, they may use your bathroom, or play music higher than the volume of your preference. Those are things you should consider before making the decision to follow this strategy.

Added to the above, your free time will lessen considerably, especially if you choose to save up costs by doing various repairs to the house yourself. Last but not least, the fact that you will live in the house first, renovate it, and then sell it, does not mean that you should not place any thought on which property will sell. You still have to watch out for basic things like what buyers want in the area you wish to buy a property and then renovate it accordingly.

BRRRR Investing

The BRRRR investing term stands for Buy, Rehab, Rent, Refinance, Repeat. This strategy has to do with an investor pulling capital out of a property so that he or she can invest it in another property. This real estate investing strategy will seem to people searching which path to choose to invest in real estate as a nearly certain way to be able to make money. This strategy is presented as a formula and there is a common belief that as long as you follow this formula, you will not risk losing. However, you should keep in mind that there are no guarantees and there is always a risk to be considered, even with BRRRR.

With this method, you should essentially lookout for fixer-up properties to purchase bellow their full value. Then, you have to repair them, lease them to reliable tenants, and refinance to get your money back. Then, you should repeat the process over again.

Probably the most important step in this strategy is to buy a property with a smart deal. By making a smart deal we mean that the property should be at a great neighborhood and a great location. The BRRRR investing strategy may seem to you similar to the house flipping one we previously mentioned. This may be true because it essentially is house flipping, but instead of selling the house you purchase, you will have to rent it after renovating it. The same ideas that we analyzed in house flipping are applied here too.

One of the benefits of this strategy is the great return on investment since your initial investment comes from the money you will pull out of the first property you invested in. In order for you to plan accordingly and achieve the best return on investment is to seal a successful real estate rehab. The first step to do this is to inspect the property well. After you buy a fixer-upper, go through a home inspection with a qualified inspector. The inspector should assess the rehab house from roof to basement. Let us see a list of what you should check:

- ✓ Air conditioning
- ✓ Furnaces

- ✓ Roof
- ✓ Plumbing
- ✓ Roof
- ✓ Windows
- ✓ Water issues in the basement
- ✓ Flooring

Then, you should create a scope of work for your contractors to have a better idea about the level of your project for the rehab of the property. The scope of work should include all the repairs and renovations needed, even the small ones. It should also include the costs you have estimated for each project including any demolitions, removals, and installations.

Your next step should be to hire a contractor and be certain you choose correctly because a contractor will either break or make your real estate rehab project. You will be able to find a reliable and qualified contractor through websites, job boards, local real estate associations, and local supply houses. However, do not think that the only thing you have to do is approach him or her and hire him instantly. You need to make a document that includes information about yourself, the scope of your project, your goals for this project, your pay schedules, and the different things you demand of the contractor. With this move, you will be able to attract the right contractors and show them that you are an investor that can be trusted. Below is a list of things that contribute to the assessment of a contractor and will help you conduct the appropriate interviews:

- ✓ Insurances
- ✓ How many workers he or she has in his or her team
- ✓ The equipment they own
- ✓ Years of experience
- ✓ Permits and licenses
- ✓ Subcontractors
- ✓ Willing to offer referrals
- ✓ Any bankruptcies

After you are done with the interviews, you should request them to send their offers for your project. Assess every bid carefully along with the information you have gathered during the interviews. This is an important part of your project since you trust someone to carry out your future investment.

Once you have hired the contractor that best suits your needs, you will have to start working on the necessary paperwork. Keep in mind that your project should start when both parties have signed all the paperwork required. Let us see what such paperwork should include:

- ✓ Scope of work
- ✓ Insurance indemnification form
- ✓ Independent contractor agreement
- ✓ Payment information

After that step, you should watch out because you may need permits from the local authorities before you start your renovation project on your investment property. Let us see a list of the possible permits you may need:

- ✓ Cutting trees
- ✓ Upgrading or installing an electrical box
- ✓ Altering or moving a load-bearing wall
- ✓ Adding doors or windows to your house
- ✓ Changing the plumbing
- ✓ Working at a public sewer line
- ✓ Placing a new roof to the house

In order to make sure of the permits you may need, you have to visit your local authority. If you move to the renovations you have planned without the needed permit, you endanger yourself to get fined or demolish the renovations you have already completed.

The next step will be to manage the work conducted at your investment property which includes several stages that are very important. Some of them are:

- ✓ Electricity
- ✓ Plumbing
- ✓ Cleaning up the trash
- ✓ Demolition
- ✓ Insulation
- ✓ Painting and trimming

When the work is done, you must conduct an inspection to make sure the contractor you hired was able to complete all the renovations you have listed in your agreement. If everything is well and you are happy with the end result, you will have to ask the contractor to sign the final waiver of lien. Then, you can make the end payment and take full ownership of your property.

The final state will be renting out or sell your investment property after months of renovations and repairs. You should make sure that the bathroom, kitchen, living room, master bedroom, as well as the exterior of the home are presentable and able to convince people to buy or rent your investment property in order to sell or rent quickly. Also, if you wish to rent your property, you should take photos of your investment property and choose a well-visited website to make sure that you find a tenant quickly and start generating your income.

Those were a few major strategies to follow that could help you when you make your first steps on real estate investing. Each of the strategies presented has risks in them since no path is clear of danger. The key is to learn how to recognize the risks and take the necessary measures to contain them or be well-prepared to handle the consequences.

Chapter 3: The Major Risks Involved in Real Estate Investing

No one can deny the fact that real estate investing can be one of the best ways for people to make money and built their wealth. The benefits of buying and being the owner of investment properties are many and one of the most important ones is acquiring a passive income from rental properties. Even though owning a rental property is considered to be a somewhat safe way to invest in real estate, not every real estate investor will be able to attain a risk-free success in such a competitive market.

Real estate investments, just like any other type of investment, have risks involved. Part of the job of a real estate investor, no matter the level of experience he or she has, is to be aware of them and learn how to avoid them by finding the perfect rental property in order to succeed in this business. Let us analyze some of the major risks involved in real estate investing.

The first risk we will analyze is the unpredictability that governs the real estate market. Despite the economic crises, the real estate market has grown well in the few years that have passed. However, there is no assurance that this will continue to be the case. The ups and downs of the real estate market are known by everyone along with the changing economic situation local or global. The economy has an essential role in the real estate market since it will determine the value of an investment property. As a result, you will not be guaranteed a profit whenever you make the important decision to invest in real estate.

Let us see an example to better understand this risk. Let's say you decide to purchase an investment property when the demand for real estate investing is high. Then, you are risking selling your investment property at a lower price than the money you paid for it during purchase, even if the property is used to generate profit through rent. This will happen due to the fact that as the real estate market changes, its value has dropped. As a result, this will cost you money, more money than you have earned while you rented out your investment property.

To learn how to deal with this risk, as a real estate investor, you should make the necessary research before you even enter the market on how this dynamic works. You need to understand how the market economy functions and works and be updated for all the new trends and future predictions. This way, you will be able to plan ahead and eventually learn how to predict the downturns of the market. As a result, you will know whether or not the time is right to buy an investment property and thus make a great investment decision.

Another risk real estate investors should be aware of is choosing the right location for your property. It is a known fact that location is everything in real estate investing. Real estate investors that are at the top of their field agree that location should be a top factor to consider when you make the decision to buy any type of investment property. You may wonder why location is so important and is considered a very important risk when it comes to real estate investing. The answers vary because a bad location will result in a failed investment in several ways.

For instance, the location of your investment property will determine the demand and supply. You may make the decision to purchase an investment property in a particular location due to its low price and also think that your decision is the right one. However, such locations may have many investment properties for sale and not bought due to them lacking a good job market and a growing population. By taking into consideration just these two factors, making an investment to such a location will be filled with risks for real estate investors because their properties will be harder to sell or rent.

Also, this area may have problems with crime and thus the investment properties are priced less. Would you buy or rent a property where you are in constant danger of being robbed? The crime rate in a location is an extremely important factor to consider when you are searching for properties to invest in. However, such areas may have a high occupancy rate due to the fact that people often tend to rent homes instead of buying them and the low rent can be an attractive deal for some tenants. But when an investor decides to purchase property in areas with a high crime rate, he is placing his or her property at risk of being robbed or vandalized which in turn will result in having unplanned expenses for high repair costs.

Another way location affects your profits is through appreciation. The location of an investment property is able to determine appreciation. Real estate properties, over time, tend to appreciate or else increase in value, unlike computers, cars, or boats. If the appreciation is low, it results in a negative return on investment during the time where the investor makes the decision to sell his or her investment property. For this reason, real estate investors should never purchase investment properties based only on their price.

You could avoid this risk, by always researching the location and choose the best one that is appropriate for real estate investing. Even though cheap deals may have a certain appeal, the risks that come after are not worth it. When we talk about location in real estate, we refer to the country, city, state, street, neighborhood, or even the exact address. The perfect location will be the one that will bring to the investor the highest return on investment. You want to buy an investment property in a location that is high in demand and low on rental properties. A location where rents are high and with reasonable property prices. This location should also be safe so as for the tenants not to damage your investment property beyond repair. But how do you choose such a location?

You will need to do a lot of research by reading various real estate investing resources. You could start by learning about the state of the national real estate market and later focus on the specific areas you are interested in. Those areas should be the ones that appear to perform better than other locations at the moment. When you have selected some locations that interest you, keep researching on the markets of those locations, the surrounding areas, and their inhabitants. For instance, you should check if people there are renting or are homeowners and if the area is safe to live in. You should also check about the location's public transportation, roads, hospitals, and all the various things that would convince people to rent or buy a property in the area.

Another risk that we are going to analyze is the negative cash flow. When we mention a negative cash flow of an investment property we refer to the amount of money, translated into profit, the investor earns after he or she has paid off al taxes, expenses, and mortgage payments. When you invest in a property you aim for positive cash flow, not a negative one which will be translated in the expenses paid for mortgage payments, expenses, and taxes are higher than the income generated by the investment property. As a result of the negative cash flow, you will be losing money. An investor has a higher chance of developing negative cash flow when he buys investment properties without first carrying out a real estate market analysis.

As a result, you will be able to avoid this risk by making sure you have calculated your income and your expenses, like how much you will receive from rent and how much money you will have to spend on your investment property before buying it. The location of your investment property will also help you in achieving a positive cash flow. You need to make sure it is on a prime location to accomplish a high return on investment. When it comes to real estate investing it would be wise for you to be as accurate when calculating your expenses and revenues as possible. Even the little expenses you disregarded first may add up and cause you problems in the long run.

Keep in mind that when you buy an investment property, there is no guarantee of quick profits or that in the case you rent your investment property you will have no vacancy related problems. So, the next risk an investor should watch out for is the risk of vacancy. There may come a time when you will have to face a high vacancy rate, which will pose a serious problem to your rental income since it can bring about negative cash flow. Especially when investors rely solely on rental income and tenants are the source for it, they are at risk of failing to pay off their insurance, property taxes, mortgage, and other related expenses.

Location plays an important role in controlling the risk of vacancy too. Investors should buy an investment property in a reputable location which is high in demand. Such locations have a working transportation system, safe neighborhoods, schools, and shopping malls.

On the subject of rental real estate investing, tenants are necessary for making money. However, not every tenant available will do the job to guarantee profits to the investor. The risk of ending up with bad tenants and being stuck with them could be considered as an even great risk than having an empty investment property. Even though having a vacant investment property means no profits at all, bad tenants may cause more problems by refusing to pay the rent for many months in a row and damage the property too much. As a result, you will have to deal with evictions, a process that is very expensive and time-consuming. To avoid this risk, you should select your tenants carefully by conducting interviews, checking their credit score and even ask to contact their previous landlord.

Hidden structural problems are another common risk, real estate investors have to deal with. They may end up purchasing an investment property filled with serious hidden structural problems and as a result, the costs of maintenance and unexpected repairs will rise considerably. To avoid having to deal with this risk, you should evaluate carefully the state of your investment property and get a home appraisal before even buying the property. Property appraisers will be able to detect any hidden problems or damages that need to be fixed since they are professionals. Also, they will be able to tell you how much your investment property will cost in case you decide to buy it.

Real estate investors often come across the risk of low liquidity. Real estate investing has to do with investment properties that are illiquid. When we talk about liquidity we refer to the ability of an investor to have immediate access to money they have placed in an investment. Illiquid investments such as investment properties, will not offer the investor the ability to convert them easily into cash. You may think that selling the investment property will resolve this issue, but it is not a quick or easy process. If there is a haste to sell the investment property it will result in considerable losses of your investment since you will have to sell at a lower price.

Foreclosure is another risk real estate investors have to plan for. When investors are not able to pay off their mortgage payments for a few months in a row, they are at risk of losing their investment property to the bank, in other words, they are at risk of foreclosure. When dealing with a foreclosure, you will probably lessen your chances of getting approval for future bank loans. The best way for you to avoid this foreclosure risk is to conduct an investment property analysis and a real estate market analysis before you decide to pay the 20% down payment for your investment property. You should also have an emergency fund aside to pay off your mortgage as quickly as possible.

In real estate investing, the value of a property is expected to rise over the years. This process is called appreciation. However, this is not a guarantee for all properties and the risk of depreciation is not as uncommon as you would think. If the value of the investment property decreases in the future, then the investor will lose a considerable amount of his money, and the investment will be deemed as a failure. Again, the best way to avoid this risk is to conduct careful research and make a real estate market analysis. Search the state of the economy and learn the chances of economic growth of the real estate market in order to pinpoint the location which has a positive real estate appreciation.

A much easier risk to avoid is legal issues with Airbnb. Airbnb rentals that are short can be a profitable strategy to rent your investment property. However, there have been many cases of local authorities issuing legislation to lessen Airbnb rentals since they have been pressured by local hotels. If this is your investment of choice, you may get in trouble if you follow this real estate strategy in places where Airbnb is illegal. In order to avoid this risk, you could read the city laws that govern the Airbnb rentals to be certain that you are conducting a legal investment.

Investment properties are considered to be relatively safe. However, no real estate investor can be 100% sure that he or she will be successful in making considerable profits out of it. The above risks are some of the most common problems, real estate investors may have to deal with and you should always consider them before you decide to proceed with the purchase of your own investment property. No investment will ever be 100% safe and for this reason, you should be able to plan carefully and take all the necessary measures we mentioned to avoid those common risks.

Smart real estate investors make a thorough real estate market analysis as well as rental property analysis to mitigate those risks. Study the market economy, calculate carefully the expected expenses, and always have a property inspection conducted to your potential investment property. You will not know everything immediately. Most successful real estate investors had to learn everything they know after years of research and experience on the field.

Chapter 4: Become a Real Estate Investor from Scratch

To some extent, we can all recognize the most obvious possible financial rewards one could get from investing in real estate. There are many benefits from following this field and the most prevalent one is that a real estate investor will be able to earn a steady source of income to attain financial freedom in the long run. People turn to real estate investing for various reasons. One of them is the fact that they want to quit their boring full-time job and become turn into a real estate investor and save up for their retirement. Don't think that achieving this goal requires for you to have millions set aside. It only takes one rental property to start a real estate business and secure a reliable source of income that comes from renting your property.

By investing in the right locations and making sure that the real estate market along with the housing conditions are moving well together, you can almost be certain that you will be making money out of real estate investing. In other words, if the economy is growing at a steady pace, the housing market will develop too and there will be many real estate opportunities to grasp all over the country. Studying you potential investment property, location, and general condition of the economy will be necessary to secure the perfect investment deal.

Many people are investing in real estate to secure a steady income which comes from rental properties. This form of income is considered to be a passive income and is a major motivator for you to buy your first investment property and start renting it out. Your income out of this could be significant, always depending on the location you choose. Ideally, you will be able to cover your expenses as well as have extra money left. Areas that are almost always high in demand are towns or cities with universities and colleges and those will offer you a higher income through rents.

Keep in mind that no one stops you from investing in more than just one property. You can make the leap and invest in many rental properties to increase and maintain positive cash flow and enrich your investment portfolio. If work becomes too much and you are not able to be everywhere at once you can hire a professional property manager.

Long term financial security is another reason why investors choose to place their money in real estate. You will have a steady income for a long time, especially if you have invested in multiple rental properties. But when you should decide to buy a second investment property to rent? You have to consider several factors before you take this serious step.

The first thing to consider is if you are able to handle another down payment. Even though an investment property typically generates positive cash flow, you will have to make a big down payment. In most cases, this down payment is no less than 20%. For most people, this amount of down payment is not easy and you must consider if you are ready for it.

You have to think of the different ways you will find the money to cover the down payment for the second property you own. If you reach the decision to purchase a second rental investment property, you will have to make sure that you have the necessary cash available for the down payment. In order to avoid financial problems, this is a crucial step. Many lenders check if a real estate investor has reserved cash for several monthly mortgage payments before they give the green light for a loan.

Another thing to consider is making sure you are able to afford the costs of maintenance. Even if you bought your first real estate property to rent it out as an investment or it was your own home, you have probably witnessed how much maintenance a property needs. This will be the case for the second property you think of buying. Even if you renovate the property before renting it out, you will have some unexpected costs that have to do with your tenants and you should also have the financial freedom to repair as well as maintain your properties through vacancies. There is a rule in real estate investing that indicates an investor should have 2% of the sale price of the property set aside in order to cover the annual maintenance costs.

For many investors, the costs of having to maintain one investment property can cause them many problems. For this reason, you should carefully think about how it would be like to maintain two properties. If you are prepared for this task by having 2% of the money you paid for the property set aside specifically for the maintenance of the property, the goal of purchasing a second investment property can be attained.

You should also know how to find an experienced lender to rely on. You may have gone through this process when you decided to purchase your first investment property. If you have not, then you should know that lenders will look for many things such as your financial history, your credit, and your down payment. These things will play an essential part in obtaining a loan. When you decide to ask for a loan to finance your second property, lenders will want to be certain that you will be able to pay back the whole amount of money you owe. Also, lenders will examine your debt-to-income ratio, which essentially is the amount of money you have to pay every month for student loans and generally other bills compared to your income.

It may be more difficult for you to gain the loan you need for your second property since the standards for this case are more difficult to cover. On the other hand, if lenders see that you have managed to pay off your loans on time, they will be more willing to finance your second investment property too. Also, your first investment property will play an important role to help you decide if buying a second one is a good idea.

You should also think about what you wish to do with your second investment property. Building a successful real estate business needs intensive planning. For instance, purchasing a second home to rent out will probably increase your cash flow if you have rented out your first real estate investment property. Do you have a plan for renting out your first property or do you plan on living in it?

If you wish to reside in your first investment property, you will have to pay off the mortgage of this particular property out of your pocket. If you buy a second property in order to rent it out, tenants will help you in paying off your mortgage, but you will have to have the necessary money aside to deal with the various maintenance costs that have to do with your second property. The maintenance costs will depend greatly on whether you want to rent out this second investment property in the long term or for a short time.

Before you decide on whether or not you are able to expand your real estate business plans, you should have a rental strategy. For example, you could rent your property for a short time on Airbnb, but the costs of furniture, repairs, cleaning and other expenses will be on you. Also, you will have to consider whether you want to buy a multi-family property or a single-family property. Buying a second home will help your real estate business grow and if done with the proper rental plan you will be one step closer to achieving financial freedom.

You need to evaluate yourself financially. It is a fact that in order to make money in this field you will need to also spend money. If you wish to start a real estate business from scratch, you will have to start saving up money since there will be a lot of costs involved and considered. For instance, an important expense we have mentioned many times is mortgage and except the 20% down payment, you will have to save up for the monthly mortgage payments.

Doing your homework is also essential for succeeding in real estate. Think of it as going back to school. You will need to learn the basics. For example, knowing who your competitors are is possibly one of the most important things you will have to consider when you are on the hunt for an investment property. How much your competitors charge for rent? What is the vacancy rate of the area you are looking to buy an investment property? How will your investment property be able to compete with others like you? Much like investors, tenants will also conduct their own research when they want to rent a property. They will invest money too in this property by paying rent and residing safely.

Also, it is a fact that nice homes will attract reliable tenants. This is happening because quality tenants will appreciate your place and you need to offer them something they will be proud to use. If the property you want to invest in needs renovations, do not try to save up on expenses by not seeing them through. You don't have to be fancy in order to present quality property. However, quality property is not enough when the location is not appropriate for the tenants you wish to attract. Do not be afraid to research and even go out on your own to ask other residents in the area what is like to live in this neighborhood. It is a small price to pay when compared to the money you may lose due to investing in a bad location.

Also, you should keep in mind that building a successful business especially in real estate is a team game. When the thought of how to start your own real estate business crosses your mind and you start making plans for being successful, you should also think of how to start and maintain a reliable real estate investment network. Starting your business with a reliable team of people that know more things than you do in the early stages of your dream will only improve and ease the steps you will have to make.

You will be asked to do things you have never done before and there will be difficult tasks you never had to deal with before. For this reason, it would be wise if you seek the advice of real estate professionals. This way you will not be solely responsible for every little thing that will present itself to you and as an added bonus you will deal with less stress and headaches. A good start will be for you to find professional property managers, real estate attorneys, handymen, as well as others that will help you in achieving success for your properties.

Last but not least, and possibly the most important step of all the steps you will have to go through, is to be patient. You may not have the smoothest ride when you enter real estate investing, but through hard work and with gaining experience you will be able to earn great amounts of money in almost no time. Just make sure you have money set aside for obtaining good credit and once you are prepared, make your move. Search the internet for investment properties and while you are in the searching process get out and start checking out locations. After you have made your first purchase of investment property, prepare it and rent it out. You have to take your time with real estate and never give up on your goal of building a successful real estate investing business.

Conclusion

As is the case with various things in life, the key to success in real estate is practice and patience. Your daily habits will affect, to a great extent, your chances of becoming a real estate investor since these routines you have or will develop as well as self-discipline will transform your mind, body, and spirit. Develop the habit of waking up early because when you run a business, you will see that there will never be enough time throughout your day to complete every task you have set for that particular day. Take advantage of the power early mornings will give you since they have significant benefits for investors by setting the attitude and tone you will follow for the rest of your day. To quote the word of Ben Franklin:

"Early to bed and early to rise, makes a man healthy, wealthy and wise."

Do you find it useful envisioning your success in order to be motivated and work hard for your goals? Real estate investors have the defining trait of being able to see the big picture. All real estate investors should be able to visualize their success and through this habit create their own success stories. You will change your mentality and develop a new one that will help you set demanding and attainable goals. You will be able to see them through by imagining what you will have and how you will feel when they are complete. What can be a greater motivator for you to realize your dream of being a real estate investor and found your own real estate business?

Understand your weaknesses and strengths. Self-evaluation is extremely important and should be done as early as before you even enter the real estate business. Identify the areas of yourself and your skills that need to be improved and also highlight your top skills. It suffices to say that you should work on those areas of yourself and skillset that you find weak. Being prepared will help you immensely when you enter a new and demanding field that is real estate. Even though you will be able to learn along the way many things, you will never understand through textbooks such as identifying great business deals early on, you will have to make a checklist of what you and your business needs.

As the years pass and you become more experienced you will turn into a real estate entrepreneur. Essentially a real estate investor and a real estate entrepreneur are the same. They are using as an investment real estate in order to generate income, tax benefits, and appreciation. Typically, what separates the two is the fact that a real estate investor is at the beginning of his or her real estate career. An investor has the necessary desire to succeed, but he or she is more focused on daily tasks. A real estate entrepreneur will be able to recognize the bigger picture and know which steps to take to make this picture a reality. In the words of Michael E. Gerber in his book, The E-Myth:

"The Entrepreneur is the visionary in us. The dreamer. The energy behind every human activity. The imagination that sparks the fire of the future. The catalyst for change."

Real estate investing can generate you many profits, profits that will enable you to quit your boring 9-5 job and attain financial freedom. Start saving, research everything you can get your hands on and start working on becoming a successful real estate investor and ultimately a real estate entrepreneur.

Bibliography

1. Ken McElroy: The ABCs of Real Estate Investing: The Secrets of Finding Hidden Profits Most Investors Miss (Rich Dad's Advisors), February 21, 2012.

2. Frank Gallinelli: What Every Real Estate Investor Needs to Know About Cash Flow... And 36 Other Key Financial Measures, Updated Edition, November 18, 2015.

3. Brandon Turner: The Book on Investing in Real Estate with No (and Low) Money Down: Real Life Strategies for Investing in Real Estate Using Other People's Money, August 13, 2014.

4. Brandon Turner and Heather Turner: The Book on Managing Rental Properties: A Proven System for Finding, Screening, and Managing Tenants With Fewer Headaches and Maximum Profit, December 2, 2015.

5. Mark Ferguson: Build a Rental Property Empire: The no-nonsense book on finding deals, financing the right way, and managing wisely, March 1, 2016.

6. Brandon Turner and Joshua Dorkin: How to Invest in Real Estate: The Ultimate Beginner's Guide to Getting Started, October 31, 2018.

7. David Lindahl: Multi-Family Millions: How Anyone Can Reposition Apartments for Big Profits, April 25, 2008.

8. Ken McElroy: The Advanced Guide to Real Estate Investing: How to Identify the Hottest Markets and Secure the Best Deals (Rich Dad's Advisors, December 10, 2013.

9. Michael Zuber: One Rental At A Time: The Journey to Financial Independence through Real Estate, January 17, 2019.

10. Brian Hennessey: The Due Diligence Handbook For Commercial Real Estate: A Proven System To Save Time, Money, Headaches And Create Value When Buying Commercial Real Estate, June 25, 2015.

11. James A. Randel: Confessions of a Real Estate Entrepreneur: What It Takes To Win In High-Stakes Commercial Real Estate, January 9, 2006.

12. Than Merrill: The Real Estate Wholesaling Bible: The Fastest, Easiest Way to Get Started in Real Estate Investing, April 14, 2014.

13. Paul Esajian: The Real Estate Rehab Investing Bible: A Proven-Profit System for Finding, Funding, Fixing, and Flipping Houses...Without Lifting a Paintbrush, September 29, 2014.

14. Lisa Phillips: Investing in Rental Properties for Beginners: Buy Low, Rent High, August 13, 2018.

15. Mark Ferguson: Fix and Flip Your Way To Financial Freedom: Finding, Financing, Repairing and Selling Investment Properties. (InvestFourMore Investor Series Book 2), July 28, 2014.

16. Michael E. Gerber: The E-Myth Revisited: Why Most Small Businesses Don't Work and What to Do About It, March 17, 2009.

Personal Notes

www.ingramcontent.com/pod-product-compliance
Lightning Source LLC
Chambersburg PA
CBHW071434210326
41597CB00020B/3790